THE BOOK OF A SMALL FISHERMAN

J. R. SOLONCHE

SHANTI ARTS PUBLISHING

BRUNSWICK, MAINE

Published by Shanti Arts Publishing

Designed by Shanti Arts Designs

Cover image: Ivan/stock.adobe.com

Shanti Arts LLC
193 Hillside Road
Brunswick, Maine 04011
shantiarts.com

Printed in the United States of America

ISBN: 978-1-956056-76-1 (softcover)

Library of Congress Control Number: 2023931631

PRAISE FOR J. R. SOLONCHE

"J. R. Solonche can pack so much humor and linguistic
playfulness into such tight bundles, it feels like 1,000
clowns issuing from a VW Bug. He can also fit a lot
of darkness and mortality into them, which feels
more like 1,000 clowns dressed like Marilyn Mason
issuing from a VW Bug. Solonche can be crass the
way only the truthful can be, mischievous as a child
with his hands in the honey jar, or even aphoristic
and proverbial like a modern day Martial. Though you
never know which Solonche you're going to encounter
on the next page, he's a great bunch of guys to get to
know."

> —STEPHEN CRAMER is winner of the Louise
> Bogan Award and the National Poetry Series.

"The poems of J. R. Solonche catch the reader off-
guard in playful profundity. While always mindful
of the tradition of poetry masquerading as direct
statement (the like of W. C. Williams, Robert Bly,
Robert Creeley, and Charles Bukowski), J. R. Solonche
nevertheless 'makes it new' through his masterful
use of understatement, aphorism, word play and
anaphora—raising poem after thoughtful poem from
the familiar and often overlooked 'little things' of the
poet's day-to-day encounter with the world."

> —PHILLIP STERLING is author most recently
> of *And Then Snow*.

"In a style that favors brevity and pith, J. R. Solonche brings a richness of experience, observation, and wit into his poems. Here is the world! they exclaim. And here and here and here! Watched over by ancient lyric gods—Time, Death, and Desire—we find the quotidian here transformed."

—CHRISTOPHER NELSON is editor of Green Linden Press.

"Solonche, an accomplished poet, employs various forms in this compilation, including haiku, prose poem, and free verse. The poems often imaginatively enter into the natural or material world via anthropomorphic similes . . . Many works have an aphoristic quality that recall Zen koans, and they can be playfully amusing or even silly . . . A strong set of sympathetic but never sentimental observations."

—Kirkus Reviews

"These short poems are an extraordinary amalgam of wit, close observation, humor, and clear-seeing. Each one singles out and illuminates an ordinary moment—ordinary, that is, until the poet explodes into a miniature epiphany. Easy of access and frequently profound, J. R. Solonche's poems induce in me a state of delighted surprise."

—CHASE TWICHELL is author of *Horses Where the Answers Should Have Been: New and Selected Poems.*

"The history of book blurbs is littered with high falutin' praise, whacky and wild metaphors, written to impress not to inform. All I need to say about J. R. Solonche's poems is that they are good, really, really good. So much so that they have a high "I-wish-I'd-written-that" factor. That's a compliment I hand out to very few poets writing today. You want wit? You want humor? You want erudition? You want them all mixed into poems? Try Solonche. You won't be disappointed. Envious perhaps, but not disappointed."

—JOHN MURPHY is editor of *The Lake Contemporary Poetry Webzine.*

"Sample one by one these epigrammatic, epiphenomenal, Epicurean episodes as if they were puffs from a tower of pastry. Savor the zest of lemon, the pinch of sea salt, the dollop of crème fraiche, and the absence of any more sugar than necessary to ease the ingestion of truth. A feast for fanatics of language and lovers of pith. I'm not sure what pith is, but I know it when I see it."

—SARAH WHITE is author most recently of *Iridescent Guest.*

"The best feature of Solonche's poetry is its diversity. Everyone who encounters this volume (including the postman who delivers it to you) will find something in it to understand and remember—and a great deal to enjoy."

—TONY BEYER is author of *Anchor Stone,* finalist for the New Zealand Book Award.

TITLES BY THIS AUTHOR

It's about Time

Around Here

The Lost Notebook of Zhao Li

Coming To

Life-Size

The Five Notebooks of Zhao Li

Selected Poems 2002–2021

Years Later

The Dust

A Guide of the Perplexed

The Moon Is the Capital of the World

For All I Know

The Time of Your Life

Enjoy Yourself

Piano Music

The Porch Poems

The Jewish Dancing Master

In a Public Place

If You Should See Me Walking on the Road

To Say the Least

True Enough

In Short Order

Tomorrow, Today, and Yesterday

Invisible

Won't Be Long

I, Emily Dickinson & Other Found Poems

Heart's Content

The Black Birch

Beautiful Day

Peach Girl: Poems for a Chinese Daughter
             (with Joan I. Siegel)

CONTENTS

SMALL FISHERMAN

I was one once, a small
fisherman in a small boat on
a small lake. I looked the part
with my rod and reel and
tackle box and net. I looked
like the real thing. I even caught
small fish, small bass, which
I threw back. But my big heart
wasn't in it, and I didn't like
putting hooks into small things,
so I quit. The only small thing
I miss is lying on my back in
the small boat drifting like
a small cloud on the sky,
the enormous, enormously blue, sky.

NO WONDER

There was.
There isn't
any more.

FLASH FLOOD

A few drops
of rain, not even
enough to chase
me inside, but
a moth on the desert
of a hosta leaf
has found its oasis.

THE EYES OF MY APPLE

When I cut into
my apple, I see
its five eyes
staring back at me.
They are black
like the eyes
of gypsies.
When I bite into
my apple, I spit
out its black eyes
so as not to swallow
the eyes of gypsies.
It's bad luck.

LESSONS

It was a lesson,
but I didn't learn it.

It was a rote lesson,
which I repeated over and over

as any rote learner should,
but I didn't learn it.

At last it was over,
but I was not the sick and tired one.

SHYLOCK

Shakespeare's only
villainous Jewish villain
doesn't die. No, his fate
is worse than death,
this Job whose daughter
and whose wealth
are not restored.

OMEN

"Why do you not heed,
O women, O men?"
saith the crow
flying loud
and flying low out
of the white cloud.

DEATH

You cannot
think it away

as you have
thought away
Happiness,

as you have
thought away
Expectation,

as you have
thought away
Yesterday,

as you have
thought away
"Yes."

NO LAND

No land
should be
promised.

No stone
should be
blinded by laws.

No bush
should burn,
and no whirlwind

should speak
in any voice
but its own.

No good
can come
of any miracle.

NO DESIGN

Although a darning needle
balances on the tip
of a tall weed stalk,
there is no design,
and that's just fine with me.

BEOWULF

Yes, it is long.
Yes, it is boring.
Yes, it is a long, boring poem.
But, holy shit, it's the greatest long, boring poem
there is.

ELDER

They always get
the short end of the stick.
Cain was the murderer.
Esau was the victim
of the cheater's trick.
I stayed home longer
than my younger brother
with our mother.

ARTHRITIS

It's everywhere,
but the right wrist
has the worst of it.
My doctor says
it's only right
since that's the joint
we use the most,
and "for you right-
handed poets,
that's the cost."

SWAMP

A muskrat swims home
with a branch full of leaves.

A blue heron bides
its time on one leg.

Four turtles turn
a log into four turtles.

The sun welcomes
the water lilies.

The water lilies
welcome the sun.

A bullfrog invents poetry.
Another bullfrog invents rhyme.

THE DELI

I went to the Italian deli.
I asked the young lady
at the counter what part
of Italy she was from.
I'm from Mexico, she said.
I was embarrassed, so
I made a joke. Then you're
from the Mexican part
of Italy? I said. She laughed.
No, just Mexico, she said.
I paid. Gracias, she said.
De nada, I said. I'm glad
she wasn't from Italy.
I don't know how to say
You're welcome in Italian.

SUNRISE

I do not like rising
with the sun. Even
when I've gotten
enough sleep, I do
not get up but stay
in bed until the sun
gets nearly to the top
of the window. Sunset
is a different story.

ON THE RADIO

They were talking
about the origin
of the universe.
One said, "Science."
Another said, "Miracle."
The third said, "The
miracle of science."
One and another
said nothing.

LATIN

Pope of languages,
everything is official
in it. It's the last word,
the final, infallible authority.
O tempora! O mores! it intones.
Pulvis et umbra sumus,
it pontificates from its throne.

WHEN ADAM AND EVE

When Adam and Eve
were old and their
grandchildren pestered
them to talk about Eden,
they said, "Go play outside!"
This was a punishment not in the Bible.

SCRAP OF PAPER IN A BOOK

Varicose with blue lines,
it could have been a poem,
or a note of some kind.
But it's just a bookmark
marking the favored page.
Or the last page she read and
never went back to to finish.

x

CIRCUS

I remember the stallion smells.
I remember the elephant smells.
I remember the clown smells.
I remember the tightrope smells.
I remember the trapeze smells.
I remember the sawdust smells.
I remember the Fat Lady's Queen of Smells.

SHORT CONVERSATION

Hey, J.R., I've got a great last line for a poem, Jeff said.
Okay. What is it, Jeff? I said
"She didn't get it from licking the floor."
You're right.
That is a great last line for a poem.
But is it all right if I change it just a little? I said.
Sure, what is it? Jeff said.
"She didn't get it from licking the fucking floor."

WILLIAM BLAKE

For heaven's sake,
how could you be both
so right and so wrong
in such a little song,
William Blake?

WHEN THE ANGEL OF GOD

When the angel of God
showed Abraham
the innocent ram
in the thicket,
did they not hear
the bleating of the lamb?

SPACE

I invite him who
understands it
into my personal.
I will not take it
personally.

CATCH

Ammons, when I first read
your "Catch," I thought
it was my catch, but it was
the other one, the one about
the chimney flue and the moon.
Or was that the catch I didn't catch?
As we know so well,
there's one to everything.

KNOWLEDGE

It's power, as is said.
And it's true. So, too,
is power knowledge,
the knowledge of the weak
over whom the knowledgeable
exercise their power.

MEDUSA

Monstrously misunderstood,
she was the giver of good,
for she granted the immortality
all men crave,
the monument of stone
atop their grave.

DOG WITH NO LEGS

The dog had legs,
but the legs were so short,
he may as well not have
legs as he surfed the grass,
riding the green wave
downhill.

ISAAC

That night, he had
a terrible dream.
The Angel of the Lord
appeared to him
and said, "Isaac,
wake your father, Abraham."

THE TESTED

For every tested one,
there were ten-thousand
left alone. Look,
it was just uncommon
to make it into that book.

NOW

Come back.
You won.

TYPO

The most
mischievous
of the Marx
Brothers.

ALONE

Alone with memory,
I listen to it breathe.
It is the deep, slow, long breathing
of one who is resigned to never come again.

TRAGEDY

It's about the door
with the broken bell.
It's about the window
facing the street stuck shut.
It's about that
and nothing more.
Oh, it's also about hell.

APPOINTMENT

Thanks, doc.
I'll keep you posted
if I can keep her
posted or not.

EPITAPHS

What will
you do
if I want two?

IT WAS YESTERDAY

It was yesterday that said, "Yes."
No matter what I asked, it said, "Yes."
To every question, it answered, "Yes."
To will I write a poem? it said, "Yes."
To will I meet the woman of my dreams? it said, "Yes."
To will I forget you tomorrow? it said, "Yes."
To will you always remember me? it said, "Yes."
To will you ever lie? it said. "Yes."

OUT OF NOWHERE

So if there is
no nowhere left,
from where
do we get the new
nowhere to replace
the old nowhere
we're out of?

THERAPY

"Don't you see,
  it's all therapy?" he said.

"There must be some poetry
  that isn't, though," I said.

"No, poor man. Believe me,
  there isn't. I know," he said.

"You mean Sexton won the Pulitzer
  for therapy?" I said.

"Sure did," he said.
"But Berryman. He jumped off that bridge

  for poetry didn't he?" I mentioned.
"Nope. That, too, was therapy," he said. "The last session."

MEMORY

Every old man has one.
This one is mine.

It was Washington Square Park.
It was summer.

She was wearing a floral print dress.
The dress was white.

The flowers were purple and pink.
She looked like a young Ava Gardner.

She smiled.
Every old man has one.

Ask them.
Ask them politely.

Say, "Please,"
with a little kiss on the cheek.

BEACHED BOAT

Small as boats go
and don't go, face-
down on the ground,
chained to a tree, now
it floats in place upon
the earth along with
everything else on earth.

CLAIRE DE LUNE

She said as a child
it was the first she
heard her mother play.
Now it is the last
she remembers as
all memory falls away.

WASTE

I know better
than to believe
that the trees
masturbated all
these seeds onto
the ground, but
wouldn't it be
a real shame if
they didn't get
at least some
pleasure out of
all this waste?

WHEN I DRINK

When I drink
too little,
I'm angry
and something else.

When I drink
too much,
I'm angry
and something else.

When I drink
the right amount,
I'm something else
and something else.

HONESTY

Honestly, there's something
to be said for honesty.
It's the alpha and the omega
of how we talk, you and me.
It's better than lying to each other,
but you must admit, dear friend,
it causes more trouble in the end.

MAINZ

It was not a cattle
car, but it could
have been. The
German man who
ordered me out
of his seat was not
in an SS uniform,
but he could have been

I WANT TO BE A BUDDHIST

I want to be a Buddhist.
Not any old Buddhist.
I want to be a Zen Buddhist.
I wanted to be a Zen Buddhist ever since
I stopped being a Jew.
Of course, of course, one can never stop
being a Jew.
I stopped being a practicing Jew.
I stopped being a believing Jew.
I want to be a Zen Buddhist because they are
the coolest.
Because I like those koans they ask each other.
Because I like Japanese beer.
Because I don't like Chinese beer.
Because I don't like Indian beer.
Is there even such a thing as Indian beer?
I sure hope not.

IT WAS A BEAUTIFUL DAY

It was a beautiful day.
It was warm.
We wheeled her outside.
We found a sunny spot.
It was a good place from which to watch
the hummingbirds.
For a while she watched the hummingbirds.
Then her head fell to her chest.
I don't know what she was watching then.
Perhaps it was the hummingbirds we saw
in Colorado so many years ago.
I'd like to think so.

ATHENS

The sun shone
reasonably.
The whole time
the Parthenon
gleamed in
reason's sunlight.

JERUSALEM

He was eight or nine
or ten. His knife sparkled
in the sharp sunlight.
"American?" he asked.
"Canadian," I said.
The blade closed.

VENICE

So it's the middle
of the night. All right,
but what a pity,
of all cities,
it has to be in this city.

ACRE

A pack of Salem cigarettes
cost eight dollars US. I paid
gladly. The Jewish irony
is the irony of Jews.

RED LIGHT

"Bourbon," I said.
The bartender shrugged.
The fraulein knew and poured.
The fraulein on stage used a banana.

AMSTERDAM

I watched *The Night Watch*
until told to move along.
I forgot my belt at home.
My pants were falling down.

AMHERST

She didn't die
like the family did.
Instead, she was
called back.

TOWER OF LONDON

The best place
to be embarrassed.

WASHINGTON D.C.

The flag pole
in front of
the Environmental
Protection Agency
was rusty.

BOULDER

In the farm-to-table
restaurant, it cost
a fortune to know
the name of the man
who caught the salmon.

NIAGARA FALLS

The special tent
put up just for
the big poker game.

JERSEY SHORE

The young woman
covered her breasts.

BOSTON

It was St, Patrick's Day.
We threw tea into the harbor.
We shouted, "Huzzah! Huzzah!"
It snowed.

ARIZONA

I picked him up.
He was drunk.
He was a Hopi.
They thought
I was his minder.
He promised to send
a doll. He didn't.

MAZRA PSYCHIATRIC HOSPITAL

She was the daughter
of the world's first
heart transplant recipient.
I'll never understand why
I didn't ask why she was there.

PARIS

It rained the entire time.
Still I managed to find
the cemetery. Still
I managed to find the
grave of Berlioz. Still
I managed to talk
with the hotel concierge
about *juifs français*.

FIFTEEN POEMS STARTING
WITH LINES BY EMILY DICKINSON

1.

A man may make a remark
and be misunderstood,
so unlike the lark,
which is never ever misconstrued.

2.

Meeting by accident,
I and the widow down the road
exchanged, "Hello," then went
to our respective houses to explode.

3.

Me from myself to banish,
I called upon the gods
to make us vanish
from our two half even worlds at odds.

4.
I never saw a moor.
But I did. You see,
it was at the Bronte
place up north in Yorkshire.

5.
Our share of night to bear,
yes, but is each an equal part,
or does the weaker give the stronger
the bigger burden of the heart?

6.
It don't sound so terrible quite as it did,
not as terrible as what this line has to say.
If I were you, I'd have kept it hid,
or better yet, burned it right away.

7.
Remorse is memory awake,
but what is memory asleep?
A dream forgotten for whose sake
we remind ourselves not to weep?

8.
The nearest dream recedes unrealized
while the others stand in line
awaiting their turn, sized
from extra-coarse to extra-fine.

9.
Without this there is nought.
This—this—this—this—this,
only this is what it's all about,
one whisper of two lips—a kiss.

10.

I suppose the time will come
that all our former time looks forward to.
Those freed from the clock, time's tomb,
when all time starts anew.

11.

If I'm lost now,
what will I be in an hour
from now? Will I be found somehow
or just lost even more?

12.

Impossibility like wine
improves with the years.
The longer it is mine
to know, the less it tastes like tears.

13.
The overtakelessness of those
who wish not to be forsaken
is the problem you pose,
whose solution is for granted taken.

14.
At last to be identified.
For where I played the game
I'm out from where I used to hide
to where I hide from fame.

15.
Of death I try to think like this.
It is a passage to a better place
of endless blessed bliss.
I try, but I try without success.

READING

A young man came up to me.
I really like your poetry,
he said. What's your name?
I said. Eddie, he said. Thanks,
Eddie, that's nice of you to say
so. Do you write, Eddie? I said.
No, but I want to. I want to write
poetry, but I don't know how,
he said. Well, Eddie, there's only
one thing you need to write poetry,
I said. What's that? he said. Do
you want to write in English? I said.
Yeah, of course, he said. He gave
me a quizzical look. Good. Then
all you need to know is the 26
letters of the alphabet, I said.

I MISS THE LILACS THAT STOOD
ONCE ON THE LAWN

I miss the lilacs that stood once on the lawn.
I miss the white lilac, and I miss the lilac lilac.
I miss the smell of lilac in the air.
When I walk on the grass where the lilacs used to be,
I try to remember it, but I cannot remember it.
I try to imagine it, and I do as though the lilacs
    never at all existed.

PRAISE

Do the right thing, and I will raise my voice.
Thus will I sing the praises of the right thing.

Bring it with you next time you come.
Thus will I welcome you with high praise indeed.

Thus will the praise be high over your head.
Thus will the praise wake the dead.

Just say the right thing to hear me sing,
Ding-a-ling-ling. ding-a-ling-ling, ding-a-ling-ling!

WINGS

Wings are all around me.
The air has wings of wings.

The air flies between the birds and the dragonflies.
The air flies on wings invisible to the naked eye.

All around everything is wings.
The sky wears the white wings of clouds.

The clouds have their own white wings.
The blue eyes of the sky fly on golden wings.

The blue eyes of the sun stare into the sun's gold
    eye and not go blind.
The blue wings of the sky do not melt in the stare
    of the sun.

Wings are all around me.
The fly's wings buzz a black poem.

The darning needle's wings sew the hem of the
    afternoon.
The hummingbird's wings are invisible to the
    wingless eye.

The crow's wings are folded like arms akimbo.
The hawk's wings are haughty professors of physics.

The great blue heron's wings wait in the wings.
The swan's wings are whiter than an angel's inner thigh.

The angel's wings are extraordinary lies.
Only I do not have wings.

Only I want nothing to do with wings
except to sleep like the swift on the wing.

TWO OWLS

Tenderly they call to one another across the wood.
The male owl calls to the female owl.
The female owl calls to the male owl.
Should I wonder which is which?
I listen to the owls teach me an ignorant tenderness.

REJECTION

"Manifestly professional"
is what it said,
the only rejection
that ever swelled my head.

DREAMS

I do not leave
them behind.
I leave them
in front, where
they beckon with
their long fingers,
bright white
in the moonlight.

SONG BIRD BIRD SONG

If it were merely
the sound of bird song,
I would not be
listening so closely
to this, the song bird's
invention of all song.

SHORT SERIOUS POEM ON
MY SEVENTY-FIFTH BIRTHDAY

There are people in the world
who don't know how old they are today.

Can you believe it?
There are millions of them.

Perhaps someday I won't know either.
But today I know.

Today I am seventy-five.
Today (Damn it!) I am seventy-five.

RAIN

Rain is water. Water
is hydrogen and oxygen.
Hydrogen and oxygen
are elements. Elements
are atoms. Atoms are...
Oh, I have forgotten rain.

THERE IS A HOLE IN THE SKY

There is a hole
in the sky through
which I can see
another sky as
clear as day.
The clouds own
the lower sky,
the sun the one
above it. Please
do not be fooled
that heaven is there.
Don't you dare.

BIRTHMARK

Another name
for a blemish,
I had it removed,
wanting no stain
on my good name.

A FLY

A fly does not fly
but rests on the back
of a chair. It does
nothing at all that
I can see but stay there.
It finds it a restful
place to stay, the same
as I do mine. It's more
than I ever thought
I'd have in common
with a fly, except we
both someday shall die.

MY NEIGHBOR'S BUDDHAS

My neighbor has
Buddhas on her lawn.
She has a lot of Buddhas
on her lawn. I must
have counted nine or ten
Buddhas on her lawn.
There are large Buddhas,
small Buddhas, tall
Buddhas, short Buddhas,
sitting Buddhas, standing
Buddhas, sleeping Buddhas,
dancing Buddhas, stone
Buddhas, wooden Buddhas.
The fat laughing Buddha
under the American flag
is my favorite.

KNEES

I have been on them.
I have been on them
to scrub the floor.
I have been on them
to tie my daughter's
laces. I have been on
them to scratch my cats'
ears. I have been on
them when I lost my
high school hundred
yard dash. But I have
never been on them
to propose. My wife
would have laughed.
And I have never been
on them to pray. God
would have laughed.

BAR TALK

The bar talk
was about Bartok.
I'm not kidding.
I'm not making
this up. As best
as I could make
out, she was
a violinist and
he a trombonist.
They started with
Mozart and worked
up to Bartok. They
left together. If they
didn't, they should have.

CENTRAL PARK

It was years ago.
It was many years ago.

I sat on a bench.
I saw nothing worth remembering.

I saw a man who looked like me as I am now.
I saw nothing worth remembering.

It was years ago.
It was many years ago.

SLEEP

Sleep came four times,
 each time as an older sister.
"Send me your mother,"
 I said to the First Sleep Sister.
"Send me your mother,"
 I said to the Second Sleep Sister.
"Send me your mother,"
 I said to the Third Sleep Sister.
"Send me your mother," I said
 to the Fourth Sleep Sister.
"Send me the Mother of All
 Sleep," I said. "Oh, we cannot,"
 they said. "She is dead. She is
 dead. She is dead. She is dead."

TOMORROW

If I sit here long enough,
I will welcome it to my home.
I will stand, I will bow, I will
say, "Welcome to my home.
Please come in. Please make
yourself at home." I will say,
"Today is sorry that it could
not stay. Today had to go.
Today wanted to meet you,
but it was late for its date
with Yesterday and had to go."
I know Tomorrow will
understand. It always does.

WAR

Flowers are no friends
to flowers. They share
neither sun nor soil.
Take these marigolds
and petunias, for example.
They're at each other's
throats, just like the street
gangs in my neighborhood
of the Bronx. We wore yellow
shirts. They wore purple.

VERY SHORT MONOLOGUE

All dialogue
is two monologues.
Listening is optional.

VERY SHORT DIALOGUE

"He's so full of himself,"
the critic said of him.

"Of whom else should I be full?"
he responded.

THANK YOU NOTE

"I bought your book,
Beautiful Day, a few
years ago, and I loved it,"
she wrote. But tell me,
does that mean you loved
the book or loved buying
the book? I ask because
I once loved buying a new
pair of running shoes but
didn't love the shoes.
I still don't.

DOOR

I painted the front door
of my house red. I chose
red because in the Middle
Ages a red door meant
sanctuary, a safe place for
thieves, poachers, rebels,
and highwaymen, a haven
beyond the reach of the law.
I'm not a thief, a poacher,
a rebel or a highwayman,
but I do curse the governor
from time to time.

WALL

It has its uses
other than the obvious.

The roof cannot hover
in mid-air, for instance.

But you can bang your head
against one, metaphorically,

without concussion,
or you can stand flush up

against one,
metaphorically again,

when under pressure to make a decision,
or you can be executed

by firing squad, literally in front of one,
if you deserve it—

do you want a blindfold?
do you want a cigarette?—

or you can pray at
the only one in the world that wails.

SOMETIMES I THINK

Sometimes I think
the world would be
better if we had never
climbed down from
the trees to walk upright
on the African savanna,
to free our hands to
discover fire, to invent
writing. Yes, it's true
that poetry would not
exist, but isn't that a small
price to pay for all the
holy books, for all the
manifestos, for all the
propaganda, for all the
the commandments that
likewise would not exist?
Yes, that would be a
very small price to pay.

HEATHER

"What's it about?" she said
 as she turned the pages.
"It's not about anything.
 They're poems," I said.
"Oh, so what are the poems
 about?" she said. "They're
 about everything and anything,
 but mostly they're about
 themselves. What's your name?"
 I said. "Why do you ask?"
"I want to write a poem with
 your name in it," I said.
"Heather," she said.

HOLY

There's a hole
in holy through
which we fall
neither to hell
nor to heaven
but only to the
big lie we fall for.

THUNDER

The thunder was
a false alarm.

Nothing happened
except the rest of the day.

MIRROR

Someone has left
an old mirror on
the road. I look in
it as I walk by.
I look like the sky.
It's the best I've ever
looked in my life.
It's the best I ever will.

TO A MOSQUITO

I know you have
the right to live.
All beings born
have the right
to live, and if
I could look you
in the eye, I'm sure
I would honor it,
but I cannot look
you in the eye,
you see, so goodbye.

REVISION OF A POEM
I DON'T LIKE ANYMORE

The woman who owned
the motel said the crow
followed me in the parking
lot because "you have a great
soul." "I'll believe that only
if I come back as a crow to
follow someone else around
the parking lot," I said.
"You won't know," she said
"No, I won't know," I said.

RITUALS

If they live
long enough,

all rituals
become habitual.

The length varies
with the individual.

For me, a week, a month,
but I'm a fool.

SOUL

How fortunate you were,
Alfred, to begin your soul
as soon as you did, in school,
sitting behind the girl with
the long, braided blonde hair.
How lucky you were to know
your soul for your whole
life thereafter, then, at the finish,
to finish your soul. Here I am,
Alfred, near the close of my life,
and I have yet to begin my soul.

EPITAPH IN THE FORM OF A SENRYU

Here is what to write:
The bitch of fame barked all night,
but she didn't bite.

Nominated for the National Book Award and twice-nominated for the Pulitzer Prize, J. R. Solonche is the author of thirty books of poetry and coauthor of another. He lives in the Hudson Valley.

SHANTI ARTS

NATURE ▪ ART ▪ SPIRIT

Please visit us online
to browse our entire book catalog,
including poetry collections and fiction,
books on travel, nature, healing, art,
photography, and more.

Also take a look at our highly regarded art
and literary journal, *Still Point Arts Quarterly*,
which may be downloaded for free.

www.shantiarts.com

www.ingramcontent.com/pod-product-compliance
Lightning Source LLC
Chambersburg PA
CBHW072354090426
42741CB00012B/3032

* 9 7 8 1 9 5 6 0 5 6 7 6 1 *